SWIMMING THROUG

Eric, Joy
best wishes
Judith Kazantzis

JUDITH KAZANTZIS

Swimming Through the Grand Hotel

POEMS 1993-1996

London
ENITHARMON PRESS
1997

First published in 1997
by the Enitharmon Press
36 St George's Avenue
London N7 0HD

Distributed in Europe
by Password (Books) Ltd
23 New Mount Street
Manchester, M4 4DE

Distributed in the USA and Canada
by Dufour Editions Inc.
PO Box 7, Chester Springs
PA 19425, USA

© Judith Kazantzis 1997

ISBN 1 900564 20 3

British Library Cataloguing-in-Publication Data.
A catalogue record for this book is available
from the British Library.

Typeset in 10pt Bembo by Bryan Williamson, Frome,
and printed in Great Britain by
The Cromwell Press, Broughton Gifford, Wiltshire

By the same author

Minefield (1977)
The Wicked Queen (1980)
Touch Papers
(with Michèle Roberts and Michelene Wandor 1982)
Lets Pretend (1984)
Flame Tree (1988)
A Poem for Guatemala, poem cycle (1988)
The Rabbit Magician Plate (1992)
Selected Poems 1977-1992 (1995)

Acknowledgements

Some of these poems have appeared in *London Magazine, Stand, Agenda, Poetry Review, Ambit, Bete Noire, The New Statesman, Poetry Durham, Poetry Ireland Review, Verse, Soundings, The Honest Ulsterman, Writing Women, The Rialto, Tabla, In Tandem, Poetry London Newsletter, The Interpreter's House, Disclosing Eros* – printfolio by Jacqueline Morreau, *KALAYAAN, Justice for Overseas Domestic Workers –* Newsletter, *The Rainbow's Quivering Tongue* (Stride Women's Anthology), *An Idea of Bosnia* (FEED THE CHILDREN Anthology), *Mind Readings* (MIND Anthology)

For my mother, Elizabeth
and for my daughter, Miranda Elizabeth

"today we are going at last
into Mitylene, our favorite
city, with Sappho, loveliest

of its women; she will walk
among us like a mother with
all her daughters around her

when she comes from exile . . . "

From Sappho's poem: 'It was you, Atthis, who said . . . '
in Mary Barnard's translation

Contents

Freight song / 11
Swimming through the Grand Hotel / 12
Tropic / 13
St Valentine's day in Key West / 14
Flute / 15
Infiniti / 16
A Sussex calendar / 17
Night / 19
The stone god of Stanmore / 20
The children's assault / 21
To lost Eve / 22
Alien corn / 23
Letters / 24
Fortress / 25
Letter in winter / 26
After death / 29
The heart of town / 31
My Dada / 32
Questions on return / 33
Bird Rapunzel / 37
4 duck song / 38
Name-days / 39
A photograph seen when I was twelve / 40
For Mahesh, deported / 42
Into the community, Bayswater Road / 43
Eye / 44
Educating Cholmondeley / 45
The Rokeby Venus / 46
Psyche / 48
House in the Holy Land / 50
Letter to Venice – to Y / 51
Titian's Assumption of the Virgin: the Apostle / 52
From Bratislava to the High Tatry:
        tales of old Slovakia / 53
To Sor Juana / 55
The visit / 56
New fountains / 58
The named land / 59
To the island / 67

A Long Island beach in summer with
        fog beyond the surf line   /   69
Suffer the little whales   /   70
A notice not to feed the bears   /   71
Uncle goes West   /   72
The lovers' war   /   76
Monument Valley: the movie   /   78

Freight song

We were lying, the two of us
on a freight lift platform

which four angels were hoisting up,
their haloes journeying

little by little up to blue sky.
And you were stacked next to me

and I was stacked alongside you
like two symbiotic suitcases

with labels reading: The Twilit Sky.
Our sleepy lift attendants

were the stars of heaven.
And we were the goods —

Swimming through the Grand Hotel

I take pictures of young tourist
lovers; they ask me, then they pose,
she with her smile laid on his shoulder.
I joke: which background d'you prefer,
sea or hotel. I'm turning pro.

Not Portuguese men o'war
casting their long limbs at mine
in the sea, not the sea urchins
tucked in the paddling rocks, those
black sweeties omitted from the

New Yorker advertised beach . . .
nor the disco, or the crooner
at the mike whose tunes you can hear
far out, sticking it to the new
moon, butterfly in an old case,

or the banquet for the executives,
each evening for a different Inc,
damp, tarnished salvers like whales
on tables, piles of peaches and grapes,
earnest women in silk consulting

their floral arrangements beforehand
and counting up the settings – for them
this is for real, their job, sixty-eight,
not nine, though all around lie
the transient families in bikinis . . .

It's really only the lovers,
tow-headed, cute, courteous,
excuse me, can you do us a favor,
that wrinkle my autistic path
gliding through and out from the beach
                like a fish.

Tropic

Rain sounds out the wood and tin
in a matter of seconds,

elucidates the outline thoroughly,
makes a mouth-organ:

wood walls, tin roof, porch,
slinking, banging, creaking, patting.

You and I in parallel
lightly are breathing bedfellows

inside this water and house patter.
inside this long elucidation.

I think it's a hundred quiet years
since we kissed and we fell asleep.

St Valentine's day in Key West

A long departure down Duval Street
of sensible moon and stars. Fluorescent mouths
and orchids. Where is my heart? Red
Loverman waltzes, all heart, red, red,
no head, white gloves, black boots,
daintily waltzes in Fast Buck's window.

On one trip out, to see the disappearing deer
of No Name Key, we saw the multitudinous
galaxy. The crickets brushed loudly
just as they do hardily in town.
But the moon in her shuttered penumbra,
and the stars, don't frequent town.
They are night herons, only more delicate.

I had to walk to the shallows.
The wind blowing without pause, the palms
dancing, attitude combré, without break
at the bar. Your moon, your stars. Cool, black.

Flute

Play on the flute
 sing my sax
the notes float they do
 like yellow butterflies
why no red no I want yellow
 up into the hills

why no valleys
 down into these furled valleys
no I know hills
 maybe lapis maybe lustred

Satchmo furry lips
 what, my Bird, what
can I sing more to you?
 Why no emerald peacock
ever ever climbing from
 why no forever

Infiniti

It happened like this on Miami Beach,
your near as dammit heart attack,
your ambulance wowing a hundred and
fifty miles up from the Keys
through mangrove swamps and ticky-tacky bars.
Grey-yellow your wet face,
then this throwaway mask,
I stretched the elastic to kiss your lips,
it was your sweet will, the same,
but dry, warm, inert;
your mouth under my terror, but you couldn't stir;
you cocked your finger up:
see you in Miami.

My hotel room, Bel Air,
at five in the morning,
I for a time as sick as a dog.
The bus with darkened windows,
airplane door ajar, panting and running,
driver in smart epaulets,
his back to me on the sidewalk.
Will I sleep again in your day's smile?

Through the window glass
white sitting figures
facing forwards in stetsons, sombreros,
motionless, one-shouldered
in the ticking bus
in the grey-white street lamp while he confers.
I look at the front, at
the tour title, lit: INFINITI.

I clutch the phone. Call tell me
no bus from Miami Beach will be
your masked, uncoloured horseman,
tell me you've no intention, no damned intention,
of hopping on, riding away –
Where is your smile –
Will I sleep again?

A Sussex calendar

January
        month of the little owls
forty years ago, that screamed from the oak-trees.
Wind wrapped its beard round our house.
In the interval I kept still.

February
        month of the moon, firecracker
to a bound garden of frozen debris.
Vegetables given over to icicles. Black
canes and luminous gravel.

March
        month of the surprising heatwave
later long ago, when we teenagers
dozed among the primroses, having anointed
our sacrificial limbs.

April
        my mother's month of seedlings,
of plantings, nurslings, dandlings, in her walk
the firm wrenching of the first dandelions.
The fox who trots to her.

May
        phlox and sweet william and wallflower.
Grape leaves in their green nascence. Birds
as loud as grapeshot, great divas in the fringe
theatres of the spinneys.

June
        month of the four noble flower-beds.
Each summer they set out kings and queens,
deep tiger lily, dark iris, red rose, amaryllis,
a chess played slowly.

July
	long ago month of the rabbits
who suddenly broke cover and leaped out from
their last stand in the uncut wedge of corn;
then boys did for them.

August
	month of my sticky birthday,
chocolate icecream and a tide off shingle
that bounced off my blue ankles: the waves
my mother dared us into.

September
	of the black strips of sunlight
I saw behind the windows of the school,
a great crucifix, and strange halls.
Night rule of silence.

October
	an unintelligible blackboard,
a whine of crying all night, could be owls,
no numerals, no letters, just o.
Prison and absence.

November
	of prayers, but still I couldn't
stop that crying, I tried to, I crossed off
the calendar, twenty-eight, twenty-seven.
Home, nearly sweet.

December
	my Dada, Father Christmas,
his rouged nose and white wool beard,
'I'm an old old man, come a long long way'.
After the gifts, he flies.

Night

When the traffic went home
night walked up and down the pavement,
bitterly cold, blowing on its fingers.
I leaned out of the window, calling, 'Night!
Come in. I will warm you under my duvet,
that flock of silk
as warm as your mother's thighs.'

But night didn't look up, it walked by,
blowing bitterly on its knuckles,
muttering and grumbling. 'What are you muttering
about, excuse me,' I asked. Night said
not a thing, but as the moon sank,
the birds intervened and the leaves
lightened their colour to green.

When night sank away,
then, followed by crowds, came driving
broad and palpable day
down the length of my road,
at first whistling courteously under the leaves,
then barrelling, revving, thundering,
till my window sprang to with attention,

and as night sank slowly away,
so does my duvet of silk
sink from my bare bones.

The stone god of Stanmore

A matt pearl light-bulb
no one seems likely to be switching on
for some time. And we,
in this pearl world of pink cherry blossom,
are the leggy filaments,
stick people walking home from the tube,
unlit, walking by moist pavement grass.

And we old sticks go slow because
inside the glass, swelling and puffing up
– we never know how it elbowed in –
a massively armoured sentinel
cramps up a genderless forehead
thick with items:
a huge unowned dwarf, a concrete toad,
has waited there all day on from this morning,
thinking of us,
all day squatting on the turn,
hunkering on the jackknife to the long hips
that despite himself Blake gave
his starry, analytic Newton:
rock-fixed, pavement-starer.

And now it sees us.
It stares us down like a guard,
our guard, daring us to pass.
Soon we will be in grey, co-efficient parallel.
The wires in its murderous forehead
are waiting to touch together in our heads.

But then a source begins to glimmer,
like a forefinger of gentle encouragement,
though we know it's only
the sunset of little houses,
we know that's all,
feeling its fingers through the pearl cloud.

The children's assault

Robins and blackbirds and thrushes
at four and five.
Your drawing-room was a mess, trashed
by Linda and Lucy,
those dear little girls.
The curtains were a rag mess, half off,
and vests, sheets dragged in, rucked
into pretend hideouts by the radiator,
your rugs driven into wigwams,
your china dismembered on the carpet,
white arms, heads rolling here, there,
the skins of party balloons
littered like so many pursed lips —

But here you stand telephoning, unblinking,
waiting to be straightened out,
calm as cucumbers —
Nothing to be done but to catch
that Lucy, that Linda and the rest of the children —
screw them into understanding —
They walk insouciantly over the lawn's curve,
cheeking each other, falling over their socks,
cheerful as tomatoes.

Remember me who became
saddled with the duty of the room,
powerless in changes.
Your eyes glide past my hands,
broken, my broken arms, my head . . .
How I have kept it neat for you two,
don't I glue your good room together again . . .
But each night those children
turn it over in terrible song.

To lost Eve

Because I can't salt your tail
or send you even a naked Adam singing
It's moi, cheri, on the doorstep
nor string two silver words to
say your Pope Joan, tell your Widow of Bath,
your Clytemnestra, your Cleopatra,
the beads of the rosary of your beauty —

All the more
shall I pray for acceptance
after the fall, of your imperfect proverb
(an incoming call, fragmented, someone
called Eve, strange, I think it's you.
Definitely I'll accept it!)

One silver pear in my hand,
worth all the golden apples hanging
perfectly on the tree.

Alien corn

for Sigourney Weaver

The colossal roast pigeon rushes
at the thin sweaty princess
who, uselessly activating her flame-thrower,
screams the famous
'Bitch, leave her alone – '

And who saves the little girl?
We do
inside thermo-nuclear griefs,
pulling ourselves out of
sky-high, quail-breasted queens,

Our Ladies –
who arc only for love,
whose tripled glass fangs
defend only eggs –
the birthing petals
of the intestinal progeny,
springing back just like speeded tulips –

Spring and nesting tulips!

Letters

The sea, a turquoise machine.
There is the letter-writer, who can
hardly lift her pen, like a wave
that can't break but runs on.

This turquoise machinery works hard.
It mills its translucent grit
from a snout of grey cliff
like an office; in the office

the sea writes and writes, smaller
and smaller, hunched, huge,
more and more crabbed, faster,
winding and winding like a whirlpool

up and down, forward and back, follow
the arrows I have put for you –
certainly it is there
written in the sand

            I

    L   O   V   E

      Y   O   U

Fortress

Fortressed by blonde women,
a wife, a blue-eyed daughter,
you stand up in the keep, dark-eyed,
moody as lichen, your eyes slits.

You engineered your prime
barbican, why complain?
We're wheat, we're hazelnuts, we're
bouncing fruit, while the sun bathes

glory on the hay in the fields —
You can ride out —
But who can ride in? Not me,
not with the drawbridge women.

I tried my digging, my storming.
The arrows don't pierce my heart,
they pierce my liver and spleen,
tortuous places,

they pierce my eyes and feet,
they stick,
they know where to go,
women piercing women.

Look at the bitching of the women,
says the grand vizier,
the keeper of the slits.
But, heavens above

you suffer!
How you continue to suffer
in the gloom
of the grandeur of the tower!

Come down, let us sit in the field
and rearrange these landscapes
and lightly stick ourselves together
with a little tickle of love.

Letter in winter

I watched television last night
till late, then phoned you but you were out.
Tears stood in my eyes. A glacier,
the longest night. Peering from
the front door, my breath congealing –
like an old Dickensian horse with its nosebag –

Where were you, my lovely nuzzler?
The blue trees were ice heavy, air
hazed before me though the moon stripped naked,
the armoured street dead still. Lights orange,
dog eyes, glazed, of the city –
everyone trying to cuddle up.

                I went to bed.
Dreamt of you. Your warm arms, all
over me, big, comfortable, I laid my
head down in your fat shoulder crook.

This morning in the fine
dirty air I went out. There
stood a young policeman; milky-skinned,
immobile, standing beside a cordon,
a circle around the bench outside my wall,
the blowing ring a rose of a white
police ribbon.

                Wooden, slatted.
Old people sit down there before
they climb the hill. Just wood, grey.
He wouldn't tell me, but then: Listen,
I argued, I live behind this wall.
A man died of hypothermia
in the night, he said gruffly sideways:
he was taken down to the station at 2 am
but was found dead on arrival.

                    You never explained
in the end, did you, why you had to go.
How your kisses danced off my thighs.
You never did explain it, or hint why.
All I had was my warm overcoat,
your body — and only the memory, silk
and over-arching, that's all I have,
of some hungry kisser, some spanking muzzle,
a glacier pulling its cart down the road.

                    Your smile, puzzled
that I might miss you — d'you not then ache
from loss? Isn't loss the hands from the body,
the door and roof from the house?
I lie here under the advice
of those geese who fly overhead
in a freezing sun at six in the morning.

                    When the cop said that,
I felt myself misted up, blank
like a furred, unreflective window-pane.
He must have been there when I glanced out
into the deepest yellow and navy of the night,
some tears sitting on my cheek for you.
I would have done anything, phoned —
whoever, if I'd known. The poor sod.

Whoever. He must have just gone deeper,
sinking his hope down for warmth,
working to get away from the bitted blue
of the trees under the yellow lamps.
Some glacier night, that was
my impression. Aching for your hand
and to lay myself in the crook of your arms.

All night
I pleaded with you. Then
the geese came, and the man was dead.
Now it's the sun, cold but clear,
with the ribbon tethering nothing.
So I will call on you only for a moment,
a proper tear or two only
for the strange man who died.
His death too must be mourned.

After death

Under the golden dinner service of the rananculus
laid twining across the overly green meadow,
their faces shiny with free wealth,
it seems you went prospecting,
swimming down under the flowers
in pools as large as your ear lobes, as your nostril.

Then they said you were suffocating
in too little water, then
it was the snorkel tube wound and tightened itself
round your heavy neck, it suddenly raised
violently, like a ridged worm.

A worm flailing: this is what they say.

Anyway you are as big as an aircraft.
How could you fit in pools
as small as ear lobes, as nostrils – as finger-nails
hopelessly and sluggishly thrusting up
through that tuberous field
so well knitted against air?

You were swimming down and
looking for something –
didn't you see it was dangerous,
fields are like dangerous masks –
in the dark you bent for something or other –

You have buried me, no thought –
haven't you? Drowned me? Obscene pools.
Ear lobe, nostril, finger-nail.

Is there a road back to the surface?
There was merely your own throat havering,
as if we were made stiff and to breathe stiff,
wistfully hoping for the golden setting.

When I came down, I imagined you
lying long and big and spread out among the lost
and I thought I might lie down with you.
But the cellars have without pause
divided you up, stored you.
I wept and cried, my throat distraught with crying
at two intricacies, one eating the other.

I worm down slowly, untying,
forcing back each rhizome, fur hair.
Stack on stack, the plates of petals
lap over my mouth, nose, eyes.

This throat will force me
with labour through endless halls.
Only patience lives in the earth,
a flower without hue, one irrevocable root.

I will find us a place to breathe,
I will find your breath in the strangest places.
I will bring it back like gold.

The heart of town

Heart-split I lived with him,
chained to engines and concrete.
Green fields were beyond my distance.

Here you wander in your old
marmalade cardigan, tatty and soft,
and thick farm boots – of all things.

– But we're in the heart of town!
Then you looked at me, in your mother's
kitchen, with a widening of surprise.

– That road or lane, I'm certain
it merely leads to waste, rubbish land,
a wasted acid town fringe.

Let's go. Here we turn left.
The masked lane led up into hills.
There a vast drain, a shining tiled vent.

We emerged like Pied Piper and child
to conical and flower-rich mountains.
Black glass wound down from my eyes.

I sank and dazzled on the breast
of green. I bathed my earthly loss
on country perfumes, and I carried

your gift, that in ten minutes
I could walk here through that vent
and by day heal my frantic desire

and still hold to my lover's
night in the heart of town.
But I woke to the traffic's wound.

My Dada

Arguing liberation theology
with my Dada, who still prefers the divine
forefinger of the wholly furious Papa –
there comes a warm loud whumph over and above
the sunwarmed serpentine brick wall, and the white-
breasted cat loitering among the lilies
flees, one paw suspended first on the moss –
And again a higher, departing whumph – I
cry, Dada, look up, and there in the sky, flies
higher and higher a circus in the blue air:
red, blue and marigold yellow, a Big Top –
a balloon, rising with stately soft starts
of ignited gas, the fire at the top of heaven,
the Holy Fire on our blessed brows,
danced by the southwest wind across
the peach and the plum trees, and kept lit by
three Victorian gentlemen, whose faint black
top-hats grow hazier and higher. *Ora pro
nobis*, they begin to call down in Latin
but when last heard they're shouting: *Viva, Viva,
Compañeros, Viva!* and *No Paseran!*
And down between rose and lily, nervous cat
and wall, there come twirling three hats in one style,
three white sombreros. One my Dada wears now
and one I wear and one the small cat dreams in,
her nose alternately twitching with her tail.

Questions on return

1: *Mother*

Musician fingers under stars,
non-playing, a bunch to a twig, still.

The evening star is kicking off
a beam of sapphire direct to me.

Out of a peach-stone, a pip, a pear-seed
she grew a wood of apple, pear and peach.

Each four stars must be a sign
and over the player's eyes, adagio,

the whole notated floor begins its
movement, its andante.

2: *Welcome*

Pink dawn fingers the postman's van
rushing in like a rocket
behind the thuyas and the magnolias.
Not a rabbit in the field in the mist,
not a letter here for me?

On the doormat, feathering in a zig-zag
down from the swan-harnessed ship
of the famous Fantasy Author,
my fan letter aged twelve
got in return his publisher's note:
Thanks for your adoration, keep buying.

My heart crouched in his writing hand.
He flipped it down on the mat,
mud off boots.

Listen, mud will flower,
forget everything, today's moonshot
is swinging up through the rhododendrons,
all over again you are here
and you are firming the muscles of your heart.

Just as we speak, here it comes
with its tank of eruptions,
singing up the damp drive
and every day of forty years

who knows what, can anyone ever know –
out of that big-breasted burrow on wheels –
whose kiss might not hop, jump, skip?

Pink dawn fingers the postman's van.
Oh today the doormat will flower,
the doormat will bound like a buck and a doe
with your very fortunate card
though you are grey and
the Fantasy Author is with the swans.

3: *Night*

So that the engraved moon silvers
rapidly up and down and out and off,
the glow tails in the amber dimmer,
air running like cattle.

Inside the house scattered your heart
and I couldn't get it back,
no I couldn't get it back.

Lower, the rain tipping barrels
against the glass, the black unblinded kitchen
and there the brick-laid passage at night
spirited back to themselves.

*Inside the house scatters my heart,
no I couldn't, I couldn't
get it back.*

Flat to the amber and silver cardboard
moon's flight, the quaking tulip-tree
like a stocky ghost in a tablecloth
of leaves, a pretty monochrome.

No I couldn't get it back.

Soaring, carrying on. The monochrome
spit or hop on the glass, the brick
lines, amber and lamp black perspective,
transparent table, azalea.

*Inside the house scatters my heart,
round the table like a dog goes my heart.*

4: Small daughter

Your white feet, squeezing on
icy herbs and soundless
with reddening toes,

you must be aware
are news of tectonic shattering
to rabbits, who hightail off
like deer over veldt bushes.

Freezing, you amble nearer,
(a pounding, a missile firing,
to their top-hat and then
flattened ears).

She wouldn't climb the downs:
they were smouldering,
they were certainly live volcanoes.

At last you reasoned
that rabbits would never
agree to live in burrows
of deadly flame.

So she climbed up behind you
as if judgement was thrusting
avidly up for her through the ground.

'There!' you said,
and she observed,
relinquishing the grand
house of her fear,

and immediately sauntered
with a grown-up smile
after the hop of their tails.

Bird Rapunzel

for Miranda, on becoming a barrister

Silver evidence of a robin
citing its case in a Sussex bush,
in a heartless bush, unbudding whips
where the bird stands astride
and anoints the grey spring
with its puff, its breast, its strength,
anoints my walk, my slight sadness:
don't be sad, don't be too sad.

You never knew, did you
– and that would have been dangerous,
put me in your unnatural and mean care,
a witch in the power of the princess,
upsetting the natural order –
how much I needed you and needed you:
there's a popular tune.

How I called your name
like the witch in the whippy thicket,
Rapunzel, Rapunzel, I am sad,
let down your hair.

– You are my bird, planted
on a branch without whims,
my legal expert in the melodies.
When you fly, you fly with caution
round into the trees, down to what's food.
Spring plays a natural tune
in which the mother reveres the daughter.

You have done me the honour
in my sometimes grey field
of a princess's flying kiss.
You sing out the evidence daily:
I listen to the repeated reply –
don't be sad, don't be too sad,
and you fly,
you fly round and away.

4 duck song

When the smew peeps out of the wilding wood
and the garganey sings on the bough
then you and I and she and he
will wonder when and how.

Will wonder why and whose, my dears
and which and what and where,
when the widgeon sings on the wilding bough
and the scaup is brought to tears.

Name-days

This name-day feast of Natasha,
her pink cheeks are burning among the snow,
among the wolves, and again Petya
his rosy cheeks the orderly
galloping among corpses he will join them.

Pelageya overworked and flirting in the kitchen,
Grisha coughing, his father despairing for roubles,
the watery street where the barouche
flips past the wretch who looks aslant,
propped in his soldier's greatcoat

as Katya leaves the Grand Duchess
on her way home to hot chocolate, bed
and a pensive consideration of the apple-tree
tomorrow morning and of her life.
The coachman's hat sparked a peacock plume

and I drank hot chocolate Russia,
avidly I drank and there was a witch
on a swivelling scaly leg like a chair,
and flowers, a golden bell and a wolf
painted on the porcelain of the cup.

And Natasha's name-day, for all
Russia's great catastrophe,
is a blackbird's power, is straw mashed
under wet wheels, always the kind
and perceptive glance of the story told.

**A photograph seen
when I was twelve**

There were women of all ages
their shoulders bunched forward,
running before guards with pistols,
dogs, long coats with high collars.

– You know now, so why say more?

One hand thrown across her breasts,
the other thrown across her mound of Venus,
dark-haired, thick like the dishevelled
dark hair round her staring face.

I can't forget these Venuses of the earth,
fat, flabby, crouching before blows.

Standing hidden behind a thick pine trunk,
smelling its resin in the cold,
my nose pressed to the barbed wire,
blobs of snow falling without lightness,
licking the high collar of my dirty mac.

I opened the book and looked at the picture,
closed it in shame, opened it, closed it,
opened it, stared at the women,
not millions, there were ten of them

who ran in the perishing cold
beyond the barbed wire and the pine trunk
(into which I pressed myself with disbelief).
They ran on out of my line of vision,
they were prodded beyond.

I left their naked bodies and stared
at their faces, and, running, their eyes
eyed me back; the small round woman
in front, she had wavy ragged hair
and broad cheeks, the next was slender
with arched nose – The prints were very bad.

Yet I insisted, huddling my piled clothing
behind the pine tree and the barbed wire,
I know her, I shouted, caught on hooks,
she works behind the till in the store,
curtly dealing out change as she says —

how's the family; and the one with
the fine bones is my history teacher
whose calm desire to be objective,
to wait carefully for the examination results
of history I argue with passionately.

Her fine dark blonde hair is wrenched out,
everything gone. I couldn't burst out, turn,
nothing and no one. Not I, no one,
to rip the guards out cold
from their barbed wire costumes.

Only that since then at the border
I have stood naked, and look forever
at these hardly discernible women's faces,
who were the queens of their bodies
until the final day, and shall be;
though they were taken from themselves.

For Mahesh, deported

For reasons to do with the paper
unstamped, the wrong stamp,
for reasons to do with your skin,

the drawn lines across your forehead,
the tired sails of your eyelids,
your hands disposing

the waste of other sumptuous lives,
the palms cracked and stamped with
the hot water – Your hands

when you took hold of mine quickly
and said goodbye, were too cold,
small, too cold, dry, no matter

how you smiled and bossed me around –
goodbye! As if it was your house,
that place, and you were showing me out.

Into the community, Bayswater Road

A beak nose and a hump,
a black riding hood
ragged from head to calf,
a large empty wicker basket
on one arm, and then on top,
the corruscating voice-over,
slicing all four heavy lanes.

All the signs, bones, nipples
you could require for drowning
a great, great, great aunt
three hundred years ago,
say, in the marshy ancestor
of the child-merry Serpentine.

Jerking on, accusing air,
cars, lorries, buses, buildings.
No one took any notice, though
one Arab tourist in her scarf turned,
startled maybe at the chador
before she saw what I saw,
a brain flow trying to quarter
the cacophonous machines

like a hound diving round the corner,
galloping out, retrenching to
the original corner, like a general
endlessly ordering, or a headless chicken –
whatever floats in the excitements
of a child's undertow who remembers
a tall humped crone quartering
the wood for her, nursing hatred –

among adults a Doña Quixote last seen,
I don't remember, she was drowned
out by the traffic:
and never would she yield way,
to steel, tarmac, petrol, concrete, stone.

Eye

Every bird sang,
only in her eye
every bird dressed
in a pinafore of ice.
Their feathers danced
like ice-floes.
Their eyes hip-hopped
like fish roe.
It seemed in her eye only,
not the general view,
some tuck
to the cornea
that puckered the lens,
some tic of birth
for which her mother screamed
and had her skew-eyed.
No, not a squint,
she didn't wander,
she kept intact
as a winter hawk.
Its talons glued to the bark,
all winter
it trained its frozen eye
on a frozen fountain
of dancing balls of feathers:
for one day
there would come
from under the raised stare,
deeper down,

a translation,
a wave of voices crying
in her own tongue.

Educating Cholmondeley

Misty valleys. Altos here can spin
like larks. We came for the grey tower,
for the Italian crucifixion, for Oberon
and Puck tapestried, thin Purcell
trumpets, flutes in blue and red –
a modern bishop's tomb, perfume of
Honduran mahogany, Canadian pine;
Assyrian angels obey, flat-haired.

Past the well-known chapel two seniors
bike and swoop down through lawns.
A serious blonde-faced third
instructs (in fatigues) some rosy
thirteen-year-olds in maps, and stacking
trestles. The langorous estates
are playing fields. Misty parklands.
We saunter past the village,

which the school owns. In the school
for the village, they toss
their heads up and down, scribbling
and chatting, all ages; there, suddenly,
through the large Victorian window
the whole bunch of them crammed in
under fluorescent strips, as if
in a tank of misty, yellowing water.

The Rokeby Venus

for Jacqueline Morreau

Running away like a wave on satin
always away from us,
like a garland or a cat curled around her mirror,
considering herself,

apricots and roses, peach and grape,
swell and ladylike smell of the fig.

'I've destroyed the most beautiful character
in mythological history – ' Big gaunt Mary
Richardson slashing out with an axe of all things,
unearthed with a swing from her walking costume.

Where you point, I put my fingers up like Thomas,
to those secret scars, first votes for women,
three still white bars.

'Because the government,' Mary stated,
surrendering in a calm and ladylike manner
to two policemen, 'are destroying the most
beautiful character in modern history.'

Mrs Emmeline Pankhurst, strapped down over
a chair in a Holloway cell,
the food tubes upended down her throat
into congested and swollen lungs.

My friend, in Cupid's glass
you draw me to the other face:
rose-bloom of all mythological desire . . .

or someone else again, quiescent, a little wild,
the skin puffy, the head too large –
almost, you speculate, one of his dwarves –

some hollow girl who looks into herself,
trying to figure out something – a thing
diffuse, some scratch of fear
she can't quite finger from her silvered cell –

to figure her confinement
– this partition – from the rest
of the body of her beauty,

the little cat called timeless art
who is daintily and in a gallery
considering herself
and lying licking her pretty paw.

Psyche

Will you come by again?
Let me hold the candle squarely.
Let me finger with flame
the wax moons of your eyelids,
the blades of your eyelashes.
Shadows lie under the damp, sharp
blades of your eyelashes,
shadow lies at your mouth,
your mouth my sculptor,
my vase of nectar,
my bed, my flesh's carnage,
locksmith to my delight's door.
Shadow under your blue-bearded jaw.
Will you come by again?

Let me finger you with flame,
finger's breadth from you,
furtive flame, answering skin,
closed, moist in the heat.
Will you come by again?

Scarred as in a house
one night burnt to the ground,
barely pulled out,
your shiny face with holes for eyes.
Someone has tied you in a dark shroud,
not knowing what to do.

Tomorrow I will smoothe your jacket,
hang you from the house beam
till you shrug open your dark eyes.

Sorrow hangs me.

House of nectar, let me enter you.
When will I ever swim
all night in the liquid cave
where water answers fire,
where flame rears to its bright arch
and cries out
and the candle sighs
into floating shadows.
Face of nectar and shadow.

This poem forms the frontispiece to Jacqueline Morreau's etching printfolio *Disclosing Eros*.

House in the Holy Land

Under the red vine where it floats sideways
like a basket of feathers,
under the blood-dressed bougainvillaea
where it arches its thorns,
we will live and be extra careful.

In a dollshouse of fair limestone
cut from the white-shouldered quarries,
the heart is dressed with chambers of ruby.
A serious boy's cheek, a man, a rosebud –
My tenderness takes up its joy.

But for all my longings,
how can I live in the house
with you, or anyone? Anyone at all.
Prophecies gang up like wolves.
On the third day I will fall down.

My tenderness sets down its joy.
The vine will fall down.
The bougainvillaea will babble its bloody
talk into the unexpected drift by
the fissured porch. Goodbye you boys.

Letter to Venice – for Y

So sorry to leave your town
where water walks up the stairs
from the loggia, announcing its visit
together with that of its sister, the light,
addressing you in a gauzy step
on the piano nobile, when you raise
your head from your book and salute water
with its sister the light, either
in a morning wrap or evening in a gold play
before blue takes all.

Sitting up on Ysbrant's roof
(I hope you'll be pleased with this)
of statuary and rosemary and wistaria
(no, not wistaria, but what was it?)
for your drink, and the town became a house
furnished with the uncoloured masses
of apartments, churches, palazzos, bars,
where the ducal sun, walking down
in a marsh red hat, having trodden
the sea into an invisible lower floor
like a wine press . . . that's to say,
I was wrong, the light had changed
and the sea was a plinth on which
I rested the shadows of Venice,
a plinth as firm as the blue black earth,
so feeling it beneath my heel,
so sorry to leave your city.

(Sending you this anyway
as an inadequate person's humble thanks,
I hope you'll note I inserted your name,
in line 11, not as easy as you might think,
not as easy as pie –
that grand Ysbrant Van Wyngaarden –
Dürer's knight – he rode from the north –
not for example as easy as slipping
on an indolent pillowing of wine
out of a gondola some evening, into a steeping
of water and its lady of wine, the light.)

**Titian's Assumption of the Virgin:
the Apostle**

How strange, you darken me among friends
and colleagues, exactly under the skirt
of your transcendence, which becomes cloud
and the heads of angels like mementoes.

Look down, this arm cries to you,
divide the cloud of your memory.
I beg you, pull this hand up through
and its wrist and its elbow and all of me

behind, my body twisting, sweating it out
down here on the ground, we are too
muddled, inept, for the bronze lair of God.
What is your body – what lost assumption?

From Bratislava to the High Tatry: tales of old Slovakia

Golden grasses, rank, thinly bladed,
naked chanterelles
smooth as a suntan.
Under the thousand fingered firs'
almighty and false monotony,
original gnomes crouch,
cackling of humans.

Smelly, with long droll teeth,
they would bomb
the dark gold cathedral
and the massive poisonous chimneys
indifferently, if they were as tall
as the candlestick
or the wind.

A clever and mature man pressed
on a plank, in the apse.
Well-tempered rivets
screwed through the spreading ferns
of his bones. Blood bubbles,
black-red, slide down
this bonebag. His

starved mother wraps him up
in baby-clothes, both muttering
Thy Will Be Done.
Whose? ask the rural freaks,
they see no one under
their prickly kingdoms, sunbathing
among the chanterelles,

wriggling like fat-bellied
kittens or foxcubs.
No one comes to the golden grasses.
'Thou' of chemical and iron will.
Who would not remember
such a person, 'Thee' and 'Thou' –
They remember no one.

The freaks are falling ill,
they are liquefying,
the foxcubs are rolling over.
The man and mother glance
off their striated marble plinth,
a pinch resentful.
Who, us, the tender breath of life?

Us? Us your executioners?
But we stand between you and –
those iron and chemical thous.
Without us the forest has no tree.
We hold back the worst . . .
Never answering, the gnomes keep
melting underfoot, away underground.

Slovak lore says that gnomes when approached are able to melt into the earth.

To Sor Juana

In God's plague of rain
– for God went to Hell for punishments –
came beatings, blood down the back,
huge vaunted crucifixes
over the whipped hunch of sinners,

(young nuns, to their wrists clothed
in lawn, who keep dying in shit,
and that eternal blood, and piss
of the visitant plague's punishment)

He beats you down:

you sign in your own blood
out of the hand slammed in despair
on your spectacles, which crush:
one lens for scholar, one for poet.
You sign: la peor de todas.

I have my pen – yours split.
I have my eyes – yours smashed.
I have my body – yours disappeared.
I have no words but your tongue.
I have no thoughts but your spirit.

Acknowledgements to the film 'Io la peor de todas' ('I the worst of all'): In the 1620s the great Mexican philosopher and poet was forced by the Church to renounce her writing. She died soon afterwards of plague.

The visit

A witch showed us a hill of hair,
a hunchback showed us a mountain of pots and pans,
a few still petalled with paint.
Then came a hare
who showed us a hill of shaving-brushes,
a wood of toothbrushes
whose old-fashioned yellow bristles were
worn down to the wood.

What is your fairy story?

Said the old woman.
The bowed old man wasn't her husband,
they had a hare of a grandchild, all ribs,
(there is a child, an orphan,
in the triangle of a blanket made of holes
it is dragging as it limps slowly
over and again).
The short and small and crippled,
the old, the young.

Who planted the handsome poplars?

Temporarily there comes a stone-coloured wall
of rain. Pigs, chickens.
A herd of roistering ponies,
new-fangled houses with balconies,
old-fangled houses.

What is your fairy story?

Absolutely solid and indisputable,
a number of rows of plum-red
brick barracks behind
two rows of electrified barbed wire.

Ever after.

Who planted the poplars,
now queenly, swaying, a kind of veil?

Behind glass
a mountain of dead women's hair.

Rain.

Rain.

New fountains

New fountains have been switched on,
it happened quickly, in the cities, in the villages.
Now how they play, how they flow.

A blank thin-faced man strums a guitar
by the water, by the Accademia,
in the sunlight at the feet of all the
pretty travellers. 'Bosnian. Sensa casa.'

New fountains have been inaugurated
quickly, in the municipalities, in the regions.
How they splash, how they flow.

A woman offering the fine red wine of Burgundy,
a shopkeeper from Dijon: 'Ces Arabes,'
she smiles intimately, 'Ces Yugoslavs,
ils mentent, ils sont des voleurs.'

The fountains raise a fine mist
in the sun. How the drops fly and shiver
over Europe, how they murmur.

A grubby speechless child. 'Bosnian. Hungry.'
A paper offered on the tube at Waterloo.
A man says she is a gypsy from Essex,
they all do it, and we shouldn't be taken in.

The new fountains are playing
and the droplets are murmuring through Europe,
and the water soaks and soaks into the earth.

The named land

I have given it all (said he) into your hands:
go in and take possession of it.
                    Deuteronomy 8

1: *Herod*

In the iron mid-air below his nose,
Masada, below his closed eyes,
a huge shadow settles its memory
across the light of the salt flats.

Starlings peck at the leaking pipes,
at the brown stain that lies for us
across the mosaics, pecking at the sapphire
of the fig, the sky or the leopard,
who can remember, back here, what hue?

Next to the tacky, the invisible
or the ineffable: designer kids lively
and weightless, between Hassid and Intifada.
How King Herod dug Rome's chic:
provincial tyrant perfumed and nervy;

scabby old bird. Masada his golden
aircraft carrier, that ship wouldn't sail.
'Doesn't anyone want any fun any more?'
Then in the desert, cosmopolis
came in answer to the prophet's cry.

Cinnamon scented, he offers me long hours
over Turkish coffee, while, passing,
repassing, I see the quick glance
of Europe, say, or America – cheekbone's
curve familiar as a hometown: kids

of a kinder Rome? . . . Listen, in the Cinerama
there's this new pop show from the US:
– 'but don't bother with *that*' laughs Herod
'if I were you' – If he were us? We hear
a peace sermon of doves implicit, mild,

with Gulf War footage, our peaceful backsides
red-plushed, the rock star lasered
over and over. Cut in emerald
like the magician's girl, mid-chest,
she has us sing-along: Peace . . . peace . . .

2: *Religious*

Across his whiskers, his insouciant corkscrews,
his velvet yarmulke held on with a curler clip
(and against his arched feet showing their washed fence

to his women veiled as he salaams east)
against his chimney hat and his arrow eyes,
teeth edged against my allure,

my free smell in the street,
his wife dragging her stomach and above it
her brown-ringed, baggy eyes,

behind his collective pram of kids
(and behind his kids and his wife heavy again,
under the scarf her eyes baggy, closeted)

while he smiles and smiles –
What can be done against the invisible?

3: *Our baggage*

(And dismounting from the plane
do you remember your grandfather the crusader?

How he tagged his plague mark
to the floating Dome of the Mount,
this turquoise boil he nobly comes to lance,

riding and riding to holy Jerusalem
across the golden brown rocks.)

4: *The other*

And another gospel of the return,
its text hidden in the Masada caverns:

the gazelle who lives at the centre of the world,
who is climbing slowly back up to Jericho.
They say it will emerge under a clear sky,

dragging its grazed belly,
scrabbling with its hooves of turned horn.

5: *The new friend*

If they will not touch my car
for five years, if they will not throw a stone,
still less a rock, I will consider them for
an independent State, I will consider it.
A most responsible, liberal man
with an engaging smile, but a cistern
full of that rainfall of blue-green
like an ossuary of ice.
I will wash my hands of the man's
blood, take it on your own shoulders.
Your heavy blood is a sawn vein,
it pools within you, it lies on yourselves,
I wash my hands in blue-green water,
this is a tank built far back
in the tyrannies of Pilate and Herod.

6: *Guide*

Understand this,
I will now tell you the most important thing,

The Land of Israel is *ours*:
we will never let it go.

His forefinger swoops
down and again at me, down and again at me.

Herod, sneering, sipping his coffee:
these Jews, crazy Hebrews, you

have to love them a little . . .
my people too: I taught them how to wait.

7: *Tuesday*

God is the intent and unsaid name.
In the desert
behind the Bedouin encampment, a woman
looks for her camel and finds instead
the kidnapped Border policeman,
bound, strangled and stabbed.
Bedouin, she is forbidden
the use of the gas station phone
so she and her husband drive into Jerusalem
to tell the police and the world.
Fatima is her name.
Accidentally on TV, now Fatima is china.
View her, in this golden land . . . Like the weight of the stars
if you put them all in baskets,
. . . view the weight of the stones.
Now view the stones that stand in the sky,
fixtures so sad they can never be weighed.
She scrapes hills like plucked foreheads
and each mute day scrapes its basket
of wisdom. She'd have better
kept down, like a flea on the camel.
Then no one, no cop, no Hammas,
no zealot, no soldier,
no one would know about her.

There's the dead man – too late.

8: *Children*

A woman falls among stones.
She wriggles round, her neighbour's
stiff with his throat cut.
She feels with her trembling, runnelled hand
the badge on the breast,
the pistol under stone.
The body puts its hand out and touches
the thin dark cheeks of children
buried alive, its other neighbours.
But they're alive, they keep bubbling up
out of the slabs, out of the talus
and for forty years in the wild
they are carried downstream
along the sewage from camps.

*

Antelope with a grazed belly
tunnelling the golden rocks.
How can it perform such a thing?
One is dragging upward beneath Judaea and Samaria.

9: *Next day*

The backsides of the Qur'ān-shouting deportees
shiver on ice, are kept on toast by Rabin.
The papers say OK he wins this round.

In Gaza 17 houses are blown up on Tuesday
for 1 terrorist. Kids throw stones,
men bullets further. Soldiers shoot at both.

Spray iced, endless Wednesdays, more rounds.
The lovely stars of Bethlehem and Nazareth
shine on all their aims.

10: *The village*

'I saw Umm Taha
on my way to the village courtyard.
She cried and said,
"You better go and see
your dead husband."
I found him.
He was shot in the back of the head.
I pulled him to the shade.
I couldn't dig a grave for him.

Umm Hussein and I
carried him
on a piece of wood to the cemetery.
I buried him sideways in his mother's grave.
. . . Until today I worry and pray
that I buried him in the right way,
in the proper position.

I stayed in Kabri
which was the name of my village
for six days without eating anything.
Then I fled into Syria.'

11: *How shall I forget*

– Shall I forget Soloman for a moment, and David?

– How shall I forget the intent of stone Sinai?

– And what of the insane forehead of the tyrant
over the rift of Masada's always and once dying?

– What stones can fill the chasm?
You talk of Tuesday, or of Wednesday, two days . . .

– The uncountable stars in the museum roof
at Yad Vashem . . . reflected and reflected . . .

my children, my children, my children.

12: *Homeland*

A grace, a calling home into its own land,
remote, grand and not today's country:
history seeking its necessary homeland.

In sorrow seeking its necessary home,
the stronger twin in the womb
is brilliant, various, militarised, lucent;

its Rome sits heavy as a house of ice
on the weaker one
whose name-lost house fades.

13: *Leaving*

That day rain burst violently from the east;
the policeman now lay in the morgue;

a hunched shoulder of lightning and blackness,
an alarm to catch as the plane mounted,

banal or simple: now I shall be salt
for this and never quite go my way,

remembering always a destruction.

The diaspora comes home in lightning,
the child rides the sewage like a paper boat;

somewhere under the geometries of the rocks
there's a print, a picture buried,

superimposed with a later shot,
but still clear and possessing shape.

14: *Name*

Sign of the gazelle who climbs up
hand over hand
from the centre of the world,
hoof painfully scrabbling rock,

bruised, it pierces the slanting tunnel:
then all at once on a night,
the ardent stars in the clear
of the sky of the named village.

                              Jerusalem – London, 1992-1993

To the island

for the Albanian poet Natasha Lako

This is when I would go out to the island:
before the heat, in the early morning –
its grove was the centre of my thoughts.
At dawn I would walk down,
upsetting sparrows in conversation
after dreams, hopping amongst puddles,
fluttering among chalices of elderberries.

But that would be in England, when autumn
mints Mediterranean dawns.
Behind the frontier you are bright-eyed,
lying in wait for me; and I will
see what I can do by letters
of protest, by arousing public
opinion. Now let me get back to

the conical hills. To my island.
Blackberries were jet and hips rubies.
They looped like minuets on a feathered
dance floor of branches; underneath
there lingered a macrocosmic
garden of weeds and grasses
still in ferocious gold-green harmony.

I lingered in the dew between two
galleries hung with the abstracts
of spiders, with cabinets of porcelains,
brambles, ivories, mayweed, peepshows,
vetches. I cast off, a mandarin
hooking ivory spillikin oars over
waves you never move or disturb –

You write in broken English, jubilantly
dishevelled, passionate, throwing
out cries for assistance and rejections
of same in consecutive undated notes,
refusing my request for a steady
address, perhaps in the revolution
there is none. I return, baffled.

I went for the quay, my boat
scraped on northern stones magisterially
furred with the past (kings, earls
and formal liberties taken by thatchers),
I could not hear the jubilant
voice of the oak, the ash or the thorn
except in hallucinations pre-dawn.

So I keep up with you, my dear friend,
in broken languages, in sympathy.
The weeds are engraved with the rubbing
of a brass tomb, with my footprints
drawn to the cool island.
You pull me into disastrous cities,
crying and laughing and crying.

A Long Island beach in summer with fog beyond the surf line

Under stunning sun, at ease
to this absolute limit of the blue sky,

tall vacation-makers, brown-thighed,
in the pink of health, brown harder.

Their eyes dunk in thrilling stories.
They rise and play ball.

Gold-haired Mike and Martha, angels
lounging in the ripples, slender

herons before the mist, Martha swimming.
But through that, no one swims.

Barry meanwhile drives his buggy,
the whiskered dune to his right hand,

the cranberry heath, the mansions, malls;
gunning on a perfection of history,

America's porch of wild sand,
hard and blonde, hundreds of miles.

He's roaring his bronze, well-equipped buggy.
To his left the fog attaches

Barry's white blinker. Just as if Earth
stopped right there, at the surf.

Suffer the little whales

And so the little pilot whales
rejoin the herd:
Notch, Tag and Baby
with a satellite transmitter
bolted to Tag's powerful dorsal
– Notch lost his while we were
lowering him into the ocean, and he dived
but, wonderfully, circled and
returned to his two friends in the cage.
We think they'll survive,
be accepted by the herd,
after their nine months in the aquarium
at Marine Hope Research Station.

Their mothers had been stranded
and then crushed by their own bodies.
Synchronous, a trio of dancers,
black, stocky, slick.
We named and fed and measured them
and they have bonded into a pod of three.
We are biologists and seamen,
veterinarians and student volunteers.
Despite ourselves, we got sucked in
by Notch, Tag and the youngest, Baby –
you can't help it –

and we wanted to jump the waves in threes
and then in twelves and fifty-threes,
unmarshalled, and generous
to one another, preferring to die
in rows of twenties and thirties
among the sand thistles
like viscous submarines,
whistling in pain to one another
among dune daisies along a northern shore
than live solitary,
proud of our separate hides;
then, ashamed, anguished, and
yes, we're doing the right thing,
relentless to join in.

A notice not to feed the bears

No bear that day but I wore
  the sky like a blue medicine hat,
I knocked at the formal door of the gorge,
  no hall I dropped by in,

but I rustled around on the sill
  of the Rio Grande (rio pequeño),
among loopholed pebbles of eruptions
  and amethyst axeheads carved by melt.

Talking to myself: Snakes, snakes,
  get away. Moving then like a shot
when the juniper stirred
  and making a derisive circle round

that one there,
  that close-castled lattice
and knocking grit down the arroyo
  into the narrow-eyed current

till it eased its transparent
  finger to a sienna-coloured beach.
A housewifely bird, grey as the overhang,
  flits between the most savage lava,

no house to my soft requirements.
  Now this bird dives
between the pacing Rio Grande
  all of a sudden.

Which stone will it ever decide to
  rise to, fly back to?
And circle. I am in the time
  of the bird in the river.

Uncle goes West

1

My uncle in London says I should
never write of Santa Fe, that it's
bad for the skin, will redden my false nose.

I don't know. He smiles me to his desk,
my dandy uncle. And you are here.
Of course I escape into the throat

of a blue white-ruffed sky, and up
into the nobby piñon, ponderosa,
I search childishly and with fear,

keeping myself to myself, and with you.
Pulling the ripcord of telephone, ocean,
on his hall of mirrors.

2: *Thanksgiving*

I hung all my panties out to dry
on the juniper tree
in the big back yard
in the sun and the wind

because it was your country
and Thanksgiving
and we had come to the valley
after such a baffled journey

as if we had been two cattle
tossing and beating each other
to a stockyard
along an unending stony trail.

3: *A good poet*

My uncle in London says a good poet
writes of the shape-changing of the Great Gable.
There is the mystery also of the Fens.
There is the mystery of the Welsh shepherds.
A poet does not write of Dallas.

Expanding over his ale my London uncle
muses on the true cities, on Hull,
Huddersfield, Belfast, Newcastle.
In theory I can write even of Brighton
if I was born within the grotto of its dirty sea.

The sea, he lays down in a pool in Covent Garden,
twirling his finger ruminatively
on the bar-top, the sea's the limit; my child, your
downfall is the plane that flies you
beyond it to inconceivable canyons.

4

I, a feminist lover of earth
in her female body and soul, have admired
old-fashioned military gods dancing in profile
across ten thousand feet of sandstone.
Worse, I've praised monolithic rows of

assumptions of feathered priests in mid-air.
The mountains are insistently
Navaho or Greek gods, Yei or Agamemnon,
Monster Slayer, Hercules, hero, elder.
The earth erodes willy-nilly; a bronze

fatherhood upholds me on his thigh.
Is this a new way to his ranch –
my father as unemotional as Delphi, as close
as Spider Grandmother, who loves to sit
on her stony needle hereabouts, small overlady.

5: *Going south*

Travel is something we all do,
given two dollars, two quid, two rupees

to rub together. That blizzard mouth
I was imbibed by, yesterday, in Chaco,

today is an areca, moist storm,
showers of fronds under a red lit

district my lover insisted was okay.
Silver moon rising and wheeling by junipers

along the Malpais, tonight is fleet
by a coral sea, a golden baby I know well.

My uncle is flummoxed by sudden shifts
but don't we all adjust all the time to this?

6

Through a crack in the floor of the grass
which widened prematurely
without telling me,
my wheels plunged down into
the apparatus of a great snowstorm
firing on the movements of the yellow cliffs
of a world below.

Above are the flat thousand grasslands
where you are walking to the sunset,
throwing your polished beard to heaven.
There under your feet
are more rabbits and more labyrinths
and more deer, as well as more
black bears sleeping through the winter.

When I woke up the boulders
were as big as elk, as whales,
animals I'd never seen,
medieval castles,
elegant towns of mud made
by past races.
All have gone. My hair is white

and they sit me down in a bar
and give me shots.
I tell them your number which is
the only thing I remembered.
After many years you were still scanning
the grass and the sky.

The lovers' war

We were travelling through a forest
of low piñon pine, their arms at once beggarly
and rich in gesture, the floor a pale grass.
Your hand always on my thigh.
The road was silky . . . leaving the deep
Douglas firs, their spirals upward.
Silence, but our lips kept smiling
and contentedly we held back from touching.

I called to you long distance
that even here in the miniature country
there is no glade or way station
necessarily set aside for us
where I can lie under you
or you under me, our lips contented.

Even here a tear in the earth
can be found. Twenty yards, ten feet
through ghost dances of mist,
between cross-angled trunks,
a delicate and sleepily blank sun,
then emptied of matter: then air displaces.

Your voice across the earth's
moonlike rim, if I could have heard
but nothing could be heard.

Ten miles you were removed from me,
too far to jump, giant elks,
mountain lions or the black-faced
crow mother might do it, I not.

The kiss I blew dropped,
dropped like a stone,
dropped down steppes
of successive plateaux, eroded altars,
sarcophagi, red and cream and black stumps.

Down rhetorics of light.
Driver, where have you driven me,
down, down to this tongue.
Who are mortars tucked under each arm,
a banging of speech break-dancing
across black screes, all kisses blown up,
washed into the red thread
at the bottom, d'you see the bleeding tongue?

This tear that saddened the earth.
As my heart labours and flies,
so there are you; here am I.

Here lie heaped pinecones, reddish-brown,
and grass that plaits its hair
at a conference of root and water.
This miniature that we wear —
each hour the sun is a primrose
and the moon goes behind the tall fir.

Let there be no edge, let us
walk, sit, lie not near
any erosion or slip or slope,
any red gully or hint
of undercut, rapidly
broadening under our bodies.

Love, let us house ourselves
in our mouths, in our bellies.
Do not listen to the soil pattering,
the way the earth is falling away now,
always pulling on your elbow, on my arm,
always running away from under
our bodies, as if too thin
to bear the weight of our peace.

Each hour is the sun,
is a primrose
and the lips of the moon behind the tall fir
stay still, in love.

Monument Valley: the movie

The air current nudging above our heads,
our guide Belshazzur
the director of the violet jetstream
leaden over the colours of the tooth, tor, butte.

Credits graph penned in
a hundred feet up, the equal dead time
opposite, brow to brow, the shafts
wind graffitied; along the wide screen, there

the finger's unparalleled writing
welded from the grazing thunders and smelted lightnings:
WE PRESENT
Cut by a tremor, scene shift, landslide.

Other books in the same series include

ANNA ADAMS *Green Resistance: New and Selected Poems*

SEBASTIAN BARKER *The Hand in the Well*

FRANCES CORNFORD *Selected Poems*

KEVIN CROSSLEY-HOLLAND *The Language of Yes*

KEVIN CROSSLEY-HOLLAND *Poems from East Anglia*

MARTYN CRUCEFIX *A Madder Ghost*

HILARY DAVIES *In a Valley of This Restless Mind*

DAVID GASCOYNE *Selected Prose*

DAVID GASCOYNE *Selected Verse Translations*

PHOEBE HESKETH *A Box of Silver Birch*

JEREMY HOOKER *Our Lady of Europe*

BLAKE MORRISON & PAULA REGO *Pendle Witches*

VICTOR PASMORE *The Man Within*

RUTH PITTER *Collected Poems*

JEREMY REED *Sweet Sister Lyric*

ANTHONY THWAITE *Selected Poems 1956-1996*

EDWARD UPWARD *Christopher Isherwood: Notes in Remembrance of a Friendship*

EDWARD UPWARD *The Scenic Railway*

Please write to Enitharmon Press for a full catalogue